North American Indians Today

North American Indians Today

Apache

Cherokee

Cheyenne

Comanche

Creek

Crow

Huron

Iroquois

Navajo

Ojibwa

Osage

Potawatomi

Pueblo

Seminole

Sioux

North American
Indians Today

Apache

by
Kenneth McIntosh

Mason Crest Publishers

Philadelphia

The author and researcher wish to thank all the wonderful people who helped with this book: Franklin Stanley Sr., Herbert R. Stevens, Ollie Velarde, Sheldon Nunez-Velarde, Thelma Velarde, Rowyn H. Elote, Tom Watts, Ernest Petago, Eudane Vicenti, Laurence P. Kie Jr., Suzanne Westerly, Raoul Trujillo, Arthur Olivas, Amaurante Montez, Robert Lentz, Mary Kim Titla, Robert Thompson, the Allan Houser Foundation, Robert Schut, Robert Soto, Rick Hoskie, and R. Russell Maylone. Special thanks for their invaluable assistance to Stacey Sanchez and Earl Dean Sisto.

Mason Crest Publishers Inc.
370 Reed Road
Broomall, Pennsylvania 19008
(866) MCP-BOOK (toll free)

First printing
1 2 3 4 5 6 7 8 9 10
Library of Congress Cataloging-in-Publication Data on file at the Library of Congress.
ISBN: 1-59084-664-8
1-59084-663-X (series)

Design by Lori Holland.
Composition by Bytheway Publishing Services, Binghamton, New York.
Cover design by Benjamin Stewart.
Printed and bound in the Hashemite Kingdom of Jordan.

Photography by Benjamin Stewart. Pictures on pp. 10, 40, 42, 49, 50, 66, 82 courtesy of Duke Wasaaja Sine; pp. 17, 28, 57 courtesy of Northwestern University Library; p. 32 courtesy of Arthur Olivas; p. 48 courtesy of Robert Soto; pp. 62, 64 courtesy of the Alan Houser Foundation; p. 76 courtesy of Earl Sisto; p. 80 courtesy of Gary Goddard Agency; p. 88 courtesy of Viola Ruelke Gommer; p. 47 courtesy of Robert Lentz; cover courtesy of Anita Helt, KPNX-TV; p. 23 courtesy of Robert Soto; p. 14 Corel; p. 20 PhotoDisc. Picture on p. 6 by Keith Rosco.

Contents

Introduction   7

One
Beginnings   11

Two
History   19

Three
Current Government   33

Four
Today's Spiritual Beliefs   41

Five
Social Structures Today   53

Six
Contemporary Arts   63

Seven
Contributions to the World   77

Eight
Challenges for Today,
Hopes for the Future   83

Further Reading   91
For More Information   92
Glossary   93
Index   95

Why is it so important that Indians be brought into the "mainstream" of American life?
I would not know how to interpret this phrase to my people.
The closest I would be able to come would be "a big wide river".
Am I then to tell my people that they are to be thrown into the big, wide river of the United States?

Earl Old Person
Blackfeet Tribal Chairman

Introduction

In the midst of twenty-first-century North America, how do the very first North Americans hold on to their unique cultural identity? At the same time, how do they adjust to the real demands of the modern world? Earl Old Person's quote on the opposite page expresses the difficulty of achieving this balance. Even the common values of the rest of North America—like fitting into the "mainstream"—may seem strange or undesireable to North American Indians. How can these groups of people thrive and prosper in the twenty-first century without losing their traditions, the ways of thinking and living that have been handed down to them by their ancestors? How can they keep from drowning in North America's "big, wide river"?

Thoughts from the Series Consultant

Each of the books in this series was written with the help of Native scholars and tribal leaders from the particular tribe. Based on oral histories as well as written documents, these books describe the current strategies of each Native nation to develop its economy while maintaining strong ties with its culture. As a result, you may find that these books read far differently from other books about Native Americans.

Over the past centuries, Native groups have faced increasing pressure to conform to the wishes of the governments that took their lands. Often brutally inhumane methods were implemented to change Native social systems. These books describe the ways that Native groups refused to be passive recipients of change, even in the face of these past atrocities. Heroic individuals worked to fit external changes into local conditions. This struggle continues today.

The legacy of the past still haunts the psyche of both Native and non-Native people of North America; hopefully, these books will help correct some misunderstandings. And even with the difficulties encountered by past and current Native leaders, Native nations continue to thrive. As this series illustrates, Native populations continue to increase—and they have clearly persevered against incredible odds. North American culture's big, wide river may be deep and cold—but Native Americans are good swimmers!

—*Martha McCollough*

Breaking Stereotypes

One way that some North Americans may "drown" Native culture is by using stereotypes to think about North American Indians. When we use stereotypes to think about a group of people, we assume things about them because of their race or cultural group. Instead of taking time to understand individual differences and situations, we lump together everyone in a certain group. In reality, though, every person is different. More than two million Native people live in North America, and they are as *diverse* as any other group. Each one is unique.

Even if we try hard to avoid stereotypes, however, it isn't always easy to know what words to use. Should we call the people who are native to North America Native Americans—or American Indians—or just Indians?

The word "Indian" probably comes from a mistake—when Christopher Columbus arrived in the New World, he thought he had reached India, so he called the people he found there Indians. Some people feel it doesn't make much sense to call Native Americans "Indians." (Suppose Columbus had thought he landed in China instead of India; would we today call Native people "Chinese"?) Other scholars disagree; for example, Russell Means, Native politician and activist, claims that the word "Indian" comes from Columbus saying the native people were *en Dios*—"in God," or naturally spiritual.

Many Canadians use the term "First Nations" to refer to the Native peoples who live there, and people in the United States usually speak of Native Americans. Most Native people we talked to while we were writing these books prefer the simple term "Indian"—or they would rather use the names of their tribes. (We have used the term "North American Indians" for our series to distinguish this group of people from the inhabitants of India.)

Even the definition of what makes a person "Indian" varies. The U.S. government recognizes certain groups as tribal nations (almost 500 in all). Each nation then decides how it will enroll people as members of that tribe. Tribes may require a particular amount of Indian blood, tribal membership of the father or the mother, or other *criteria*. Some enrolled tribal members who are legally "Indian" may not look Native at all; many have blond hair and blue eyes and others have clearly African features. At the same time, there are thousands of Native people whose tribes have not yet been officially recognized by the government.

We have done our best to write books that are as free from stereotypes as possible. But you as the reader also play a part. After reading one of these books, we hope you won't think: "The Cheyenne are all like this" or "Iroquois are all like that." Each person in this world is unique, whatever their culture. Stereotypes shut people's minds—but these books are intended to open your mind. North American Indians today have much wisdom and beauty to offer.

Some people consider American Indians to be a historical topic only, but Indians today are living, contributing members of North American society. The contributions of the various Indian cultures enrich our world—and North America would be a very different place without the Native people who live there. May they never be lost in North America's "big, wide river"!

A Native artist's interpretation of a mountain spirit, one of the beings described by Apache oral traditions.

Chapter 1

Beginnings

DĀANZHO!
("Welcome!" in Jicarilla Apache dialect.)

When I was a boy, if someone said the word "Apache" my mind would jump to a picture of a frightening, whooping, painted warrior. The Apaches were the villains of Wild West TV shows; they were ferocious and untamable. Today, when I think of Apache people, however, I remember a relaxed visit with a kindhearted man who loves the peaceful stillness of a country night. Or I think of the confident, well-educated woman who proudly explained to me the accomplishments of her Indian nation over the past decade. And I recall laughing with a talented cartoonist who was drawing his idea of what would happen if Osama Bin Laden tried to hide out on his people's reservation.

Few groups of Indians have become so famous—or so badly stereotyped—as the Apache. Their name has become an expression for savage behavior. Yet historically, the Apache were not unusually warlike. Some fought

Herbert Stevens is manager at the San Carlos Apache Cultural Center, off Highway 70 in Arizona. Guests to the cultural center can gain unique insights into Western Apache ways.

bravely to defend their people. Others tried to live peacefully, even when whites and other tribes mistreated them.

We are also mistaken if we think of the Apache as a single tribe. Instead, they are diverse groups of people. They share somewhat similar Ndee languages, yet have many different customs and histories.

Perhaps the biggest misunderstanding is the idea that Apache people disappeared after white settlers moved West. The Apache exist in many people's minds as pictures from history, not as modern-day fellow citizens. Yet, on the 2000 national census, 96,000 people identified themselves as Apache.

In order to understand the various Apache peoples today, we need to go back to their beginning. Archaeologists look at stones and bones to guess at these things, but *traditional* Apache have their own understanding of the past. These traditions vary from tribe to tribe, and differences exist even within the same tribe. Here is a Chiricahua account of ancient times.

In the beginning the world was covered with darkness; there was no sunshine. But there were all kinds of creatures—birds, deer, antelope, squirrels, and lizards were there just like today. There were also enormous, terrible monsters. People could not live under such conditions, for the monsters ate all human offspring.

The animals had two tribes—the birds and the beasts—and they could think and speak like humans do now.

The birds were tired of darkness; they wanted light in their world. But the other tribe steadfastly refused. The beasts liked perpetual nighttime. So the birds warred against the beasts. The ground creatures fought with clubs, but the eagle had taught the birds how to shoot bows and arrows.

Now the snakes were so wise they could not be killed. One snake hid in the side of a mountain in Arizona, and his eyes (changed into a brilliant stone) may be seen in the rock there today. A great monster could not be killed either, for he was covered with four layers of bone scales. Arrows just bounced off his skin.

It was a terrible battle, but the birds had the advantage of flight. They flew above their enemies and dropped large stones on them. After many days, the birds won.

When the war was over, some evil creatures still remained, but the birds had control of the world. They allowed light to come into the world. The eagle was the chief of the birds in their battle for light, and that is why even today his feathers are worn as emblems of wisdom, justice, and power.

A woman lived on the earth named White Painted Woman. She could outwit most animals except for the great monster, which was very wise and very evil, and would come and eat her babies. The beast had devoured all her children.

White Painted Woman prayed for deliverance. As she did so, rain fell down upon her. She reached up to embrace the rain, and the rain conceived a child within her. When her son was about to be born, she dug a deep cave in which to hide him. She gave birth to a boy and named him Child of Water.

White Painted Woman built a fire that hid the entrance to the cave and kept her baby warm. Each day, she would extinguish the fire to nurse him in the cave, and then light it again when she left.

In this Chiricahua account, Child of Water stands alone as the hero. In the sacred traditions of the Western Apaches, Lipan, and Jicarilla Apaches, White Painted Woman bears two sons. Killer of Enemies is fathered by the Sun and Child of Water is born of Rain. These hero twins then rid the earth of monsters.

In Chiricahua sacred history, the eagle was chief of the birds in the battle to bring light into the world.

When the child grew older he didn't want to stay in the cave; he wanted to run and play outside, and so he would venture out while his mother was gone. The monster saw the child's tracks. He knew they belonged to a tasty young human, and he was frustrated he couldn't find the child. If the mother did not reveal her child's whereabouts, he threatened, he would kill her. The poor mother didn't know what to do; she could not betray her child, but she couldn't stand up against the monster.

One morning Child of Water announced he was old enough to go hunting. His mother begged him not to, but he had made up his mind.

The only man alive then was the boy's uncle, and he showed Child of Water how to make a bow and sharp stone-tipped arrows. The uncle led the boy into the hills, where the older man taught the younger how to stalk wary deer. After a few days, Child of Water shot a buck, his arrow passing right through the creature's heart. His uncle taught him how to skin the deer and remove the best meat. They broiled two hindquarters, one for

Child of Water and one for his uncle. The monster smelled the delicious meat cooking and came right up to the two men. The uncle was paralyzed with fear, but Child of Water boldly stood his ground.

The monster snatched up the stick that held the boy's piece of meat and sat down to eat it. He said to the young man: "You are just what I have been looking for—a nice, fat, delicious boy. So after I have eaten this venison I shall eat you."

The boy said, "No! You won't eat me or my meat." He grabbed the venison off the branch and returned to where he had been sitting by the fire.

The monster said, "You certainly are brave—but foolish. What do you think you can do against a great creature like me?"

Child of Water replied, "I can defend myself perfectly well; as you may soon find out."

The monster snatched the meat back, and the boy grabbed it back again.

"I dare you to fight me," the boy said.

"I'll fight you any way you want."

"We'll stand a hundred feet apart," the boy answered, "and exchange shots with our bows and arrows. You can take four shots first. If you miss, I get four shots at you."

The monster was overjoyed, anticipating how good the young man would taste after he killed him.

The monster's bow was made out of a tall pine tree, and his arrows were made from saplings, each twenty feet long. He aimed carefully, but at the instant he released his arrow the boy made a loud sound and jumped into the air. The arrow flew into splinters in midair, and the boy appeared standing on the top of a bright rainbow over the spot at which the monster had aimed. Then the rainbow disappeared and the boy was standing on the ground again. This happened three more times.

Now it was the young man's turn to shoot. The monster taunted him: "Your little arrows cannot pierce even one coat of horn, and I have three other coats—so fire away!" The

The Yavapai-Apache Creation tradition is a little different from that of other Apache tribes. The hero's name is Sakarakaamche, and he kills a giant eagle. After that, Sakarakaamche desires a wife, but has no one to marry. While thinking about this problem, Sakarakaamche plays with a lump of clay. He absentmindedly forms a likeness of his mother. Pleased, he makes more clay figures. He closes his eyes and dreams of a canyon full of people. When he opens his eyes, the clay figures have come to life. That's where the Native people of this land came from.

Sunrise comes over a hill in New Mexico's Jicarilla Nation. After the birds triumphed over the other creatures, light was allowed to illuminate the earth.

boy's first arrow hit just over the monster's heart, and one scale fell to the ground. The next arrow hit in the same place, and another enormous green scale fell. The third shot did the same. Now the monster's heart was exposed.

Before releasing his fourth shot, Child of Water yelled: "Uncle! Run from that spot, or the monster will fall upon you." His uncle found courage and sprinted away from the monster's shadow. The young man's arrow swooshed into the air and flew straight into the monster's heart. The monster screamed; the earth shook as he rolled in agony. The gigantic beast crashed into the side of a mountain and rolled down, dead, into the canyon below.

Suddenly, dark clouds swept in, lightning crashed, and rains poured down. When the storm passed, the young man and his uncle could see fragments of the huge body of the monster lying among the rocks. The bones of this monster may be seen there today.

Usen, the Creator, taught the young man how to prepare herbs for medicine, how to hunt, and how to fight. More people were created, and Child of Water became their chief. Usen gave the people a homeland—mountains full of game, forests, streams, and lakes. Some Apache have now been driven far from their ancestral home, while others still live on portions of their old grounds.

This bow and arrow set from the old days, displayed at the San Carlos Apache Cultural Center, is reminiscent of Child of Water's weapons. Even after they had firearms, Apache men were highly skilled archers. The bow could be both silent and deadly for hunting and warfare.

More than a century ago, photographer Edward Curtis took this picture of Apache men "storytelling." Sacred traditions and cultural history were passed down for many centuries by word of mouth. The most important Apache spiritual beliefs are still passed on by oral tradition, rather than written down.

Woven bowls in the San Carlos Apache Cultural Center demonstrate the highly sophisticated artistic skills of the Western Apache traditional cultures.

Chapter 2

History

It's funny what you do and don't read in "history." Most of the numerous historical articles about Apache on the Internet refer to the "warlike" nature of the tribe. But very few tell about the Camp Grant Massacre.

In the early months of 1871, people living in Arizona—white settlers, Latinos, and Indians—all suffered from drought. Facing starvation, the Aravaipa Apache raided a supply train. Enraged citizens of Tucson formed a *vigilante* group. This mixed group of Anglos, Latinos, and Papago Indians came upon a sleeping camp of Apache. In less than thirty minutes, eight men and 110 women and children were brutally murdered. Twenty-eight babies were taken and sold to Mexican slave traders. Months later, a mock trial was held. No one was found guilty for the killings.

Many white people might be tempted to forget such things, but the Western Apache have not. One gentleman in the tribe still tells the story about when his grandparents were part of the same band that was massacred. They had been warned by a *medicine man* that something awful was going

Some Apache groups, like the Llanero band of the Jicarillas and the Kiowa Apaches, lived in tepees, which were well suited to a nomadic life following bison herds.

to happen, so they left before the attack. From some perspectives, when we look at the "big picture" of the Apaches and their encounters with non-Indian culture, the Apaches appear to be the less "savage" of the two.

The name "Apache" is actually a Zuni word meaning "enemy." In their own language, the Apache call themselves *Ndee*—"the People." The language group common to Apache is Athapaskan. Scientists theorize the original Ndee left a larger group of Athapaskan speaking people in Canada and moved into the southwestern United States around A.D. 800. The Ndee disagree with this, however; they believe they have always lived in the Southwest.

By 1700 there were seven major groups of people speaking Apache languages:

- the Mescalero Apache
- the Lipan Apache
- the Kiowa Apache
- the Jicarilla Apache

- the Chiricahua Apache
- the Navajo
- the Western Apache

Each group had distinct customs, beliefs, and ways of living. The groups were divided into a number of smaller groups. These could include as many as thirty extended families, or two hundred people. The local groups sometimes joined together to form larger units commonly referred to as "bands." When making wars or treaties with the Apache, *Westerners* frequently confused one group of Apache for another.

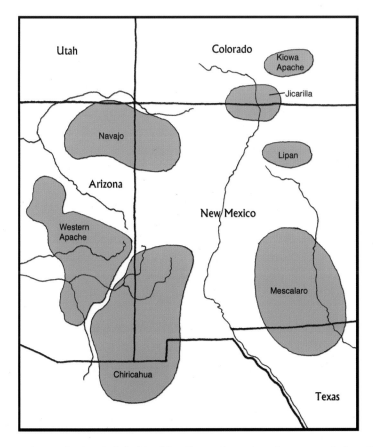

This map shows the lands inhabited by the various Apache groups before the European invasion.

The Mescalero, the easternmost Apache group, were buffalo hunters. They also used the *mescal* plant, from which they got their name.

Early in the 1700s, Comanche and Ute tribes repeatedly attacked the Mescalero. The Mescalero made treaties with the Spanish government to stand together against these tribes. They moved close to Spanish forts and made trade agreements in exchange for protection.

In 1848, the United States took control of New Mexico. Unfortunately, the government failed to distinguish between groups of Apaches. Conflicts with other tribes led to war against the Mescalero. In 1862, Kit Carson was told to take troops and "kill Mescalero men wherever you find them." This military campaign led to a decade of miserable captivity for the Mescalero at Fort Sumner.

In 1873, they were given their present-day *reservation* lands in southern New Mexico. Life on the reservation was very difficult at first. On the reservation land, the Mescalero were forced to depend on the government for food and survival. The food was frequently neglected or sold by greedy agents to non-Indians. Withholding food was used as a weapon against families who tried to retain traditional ways. Along with hunger, *smallpox* swept through the reservation, killing many.

The Indian Reorganization Act, also known as "the Indian New Deal," was enacted in 1934. This changed federal policy toward all Indian tribes. It ended full-scale attempts to stamp out Indian culture and encouraged tribes to develop their own governments and businesses. The Mescalero began to move ahead with farming and ranching.

From 1955 until 1998, Wendell Chino served as business council chairman, then as the first president of the Mescalero Apache. Under his firm leadership, the Mescalero developed a ski resort, lumber industry, inn, and casino. The Mescalero Nation today is strong economically due to these developments.

The Lipan Apache have their own history. Their name means "Mountain Warriors." Originally they were closely related to the Jicarilla, but after they acquired horses from the Spanish around 1700, the Lipan separated from the Jicarilla and moved south, down into Texas, to trade and hunt buffalo. They attempted to join with the Spanish against the Comanches, but Spanish forces proved unable to help them.

In 1846, the Lipan chose to fight with Texan forces against Mexico. Tragically, after statehood was won, Texas settlers undertook the extermination of all Indians in the state—including their former Lipan allies. Some

The Robert Soto Family are Lipan Apaches living in Texas. They dance and share their Lipan culture around the world.

Lipans moved in with the Mescalero, and many Lipan Apache are part of the Mescalero Apache Nation today. Others fled south to Mexico, where they stayed among the Kickapoo.

In the early twentieth century, the Lipan Apache moved back to Texas. Small bands have always been more important to the Lipan than a larger tribal unit. Bands settled together in San Antonio, McAllen, Laredo, and Victoria, Texas. Today, almost six hundred Lipan are known to reside in Texas. They have petitioned the state of Texas and the federal government for recognition of their tribal status.

Another band of Lipan Apache was sold as slaves to the French and taken to Louisiana. They joined with the Choctaws there and are now known as the Choctaw-Lipan Apache Tribe. They have been officially recognized by the state of Louisiana but not by the federal government.

Originally, the Plains Apache were part of another Apache band. In the 1700s, they allied with the Kiowas for strength against common enemies. They lived in tepees in western Kansas, hunted buffalo, and lived in ways similar to their Kiowa brethren. Over the next hundred years, French and Spanish traders brought horses and guns to the Indians. They also brought diseases, which killed many of the tribe.

In 1867, the Medicine Lodge Treaty established a reservation for the Arapaho, Cheyenne, Comanche, and Plains Apache in Oklahoma. Conditions on the reservation were terrible. After government policy dissolved the reservation in 1902, most of the land was purchased by non-Native people.

In 1972, the Plains Apache formally organized a tribal government. They are now known as the Apache Tribe of Oklahoma. Their government offices are in the town of Anadarko. This area offers the tribe few financial opportunities, yet the Plains Apache keep their distinctive cultural traditions alive. Their ceremonies include the giving of an Apache name to children, and Blackfeet and Rabbit dances.

The name Jicarilla (pronounced "hee-ka-ree-ya") is Spanish; it means, literally, "little basket," but may imply "little basket maker," referring to the Jicarilla's finely woven baskets, or "chocolate cup" referring to the color of their beautiful pottery. Their own tribal name is *Tinde*, which means "people of the mountains."

Originally, the Jicarilla were two distinct groups. The Llanero were buffalo hunters, living in tepees and hunting buffalo like the Plains Indian tribes. The Ollero were farmers who lived in settled villages more like the Pueblo Indians. Notice the map showing the extent of their ancestral lands compared to their reservation today (page 26).

In the 1700s, the Jicarilla made treaties with the Spanish to fight together against Comanche foes. Even today, the Jicarilla have friendships and marriages with their Latino neighbors.

After the American government took control of New Mexico, relationships between Anglos and Indians were strained. As Veronica Tiller says in her book *The Jicarilla Apache Tribe*, American policy was "governed by the needs of the white population, whose overriding desire was to push the Indians out of the path of settlement and then keep them out at minimum expense." In 1873, the Jicarilla were forced to move south to the Mescalero Reservation. At this same time, the Ollero and Llanero joined together politically to advance their common cause.

By 1887, they were allowed to resettle on a tiny portion of their homeland. The Jicarilla developed a timber industry, but corrupt federal agents

A San Carlos Apache girl's doll in the San Carlos Apache Cultural Center. She wears a traditional buckskin dress with tinklers made from old tobacco tins.

stole their profits. Government policies and mismanagement caused massive poverty and despair on the reservation into the 1930s. ***Tuberculosis epidemics*** swept through time and again, killing hundreds of people.

The Indian Reorganization Act of 1934 began an era of new opportunity. The Jicarilla were fortunate to have some extremely talented leaders who focused on education and business development. Sheep and then oil became the basis of tribal economy. The Jicarilla were the first tribe to invest in the stock market. At the start of the twenty-first century, they are one of the economically strongest Indian Nations in the country. They continue to live their distinctly Apache beliefs and culture.

The Chiricahua originally lived by farming, hunting, gathering wild foods, and trading with nearby Pueblo Indians. In the 1600s, Spanish slave traders raided them, but the Chiricahua fought back. In the early 1800s, the Mexican government offered a hundred pesos for each Apache man's scalp, fifty pesos for each woman's, and twenty-five pesos for each child's. This attempted *genocide* forced the Chiricahua to wage bitter war.

In 1858, a Chiricahua warrior named Goyahkla and his band accepted an offer to trade with Mexican troops near the town of Janos. The offer was a trick. Mexican soldiers attacked, killing 130 Apache—mostly women and

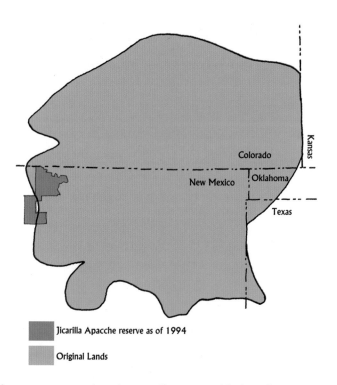

Jicarilla Apacche reserve as of 1994

Original Lands

Compare the vast expanse that the Jicarillas roamed before the European invasion with the size of their nation today.

children—and enslaving eighty more. Goyahkla lost his mother, wife, and children.

Driven by bitter grief, over the next few years Goyahkla fought hard against the Mexicans. Mexican troops became so afraid of him they would call out, "Saint Geronimo save us!" when he approached—hence Goyahkla became known as Geronimo.

In the early 1860s, Magnas Coloradas and Cochise, both of whom were leaders of southern Apache bands, suffered from unprovoked attacks by Anglo settlers. For the next two decades, Chiricahua leaders were forced time and again to fight for their lands and families. Geronimo's last campaign became legendary, as he and his thirty-seven men eluded a quarter of the entire U.S. army.

After their eventual surrender in 1886, all the Chiricahua men—even scouts who had loyally served the U.S. army—were sent to prison in Florida. They were then kept at Fort Sill, Oklahoma, where many died. Over thirty-three years, an entire Indian nation was held hostage.

Finally, in 1913, the Chiricahua were granted their freedom from Fort Sill—but they were not given a reservation. Most of them went to live with the Mescalero, and today they are part of the Mescalero Apache Nation. About a hundred Chiricahua remained in Oklahoma. They suffered badly during the next decade, as they were forced to move away from their cattle.

During the 1950s, the U.S. federal government proposed doing away with official recognition of the Fort Sill Apache. This forced the people to become more strongly organized. In 1976, they adopted a formal **constitution**. Tourists and tribal government offices employ some tribal members, yet the Fort Sill Apache are still working to develop more jobs for their nation.

Navajo is closely related to the Apache language family, but culturally they are distinct from the Apaches. *Navajo* is a Pueblo Indian word that means "planted fields." This tribe calls themselves Diné—"the people." (To learn more about the Navajo-Diné today, read *Navajo*, another title in the North American Indians Today series.)

A number of Apache tribes and bands have been lumped together under the term "Western Apache," but there are definite differences between them. The San Carlos, White Mountain, Tonto, and Cibecue Apache are some of the largest groups. The Verde Valley Apache should also be included.

Before meeting Europeans, these were peaceful traders and farmers.

Goyahkla, better known as Geronimo, was portrayed by American and European novelists and reporters as a ferocious fighter. In fact, he was a man who knew deep sadness after seeing his family murdered and lands invaded first by Mexicans, then by Anglo-Americans. He spent much of his life trying to defend his people from annihilation.

Due to their location, they did not meet up with Europeans until around 1700. White Mountain Apache continued to live relatively peaceful lives for another century. In 1863, however, gold was discovered at Prescott, Arizona, in the heart of Tonto Apache lands. The Apache fought for eight years against the hordes of trespassing miners. In 1871, Tucson citizens massacred a group of San Carlos (Aravaipa), mostly women and children.

After this, the U.S. government announced its so called "peace policy," which meant rounding up all the Western Apache along with some Chiricahua onto what is now the San Carlos Reservation. Like other such efforts, it was a disaster. Without any means of food production, Apache on the overcrowded reservation were completely dependent on government handouts. Uncaring or dishonest agents often failed to deliver promised food and clothing. What the government termed "outbreaks" were often Apaches sneaking out of the reservation boundaries in order to hunt food for their starving families.

Longing for an End to Captivity

"There is a great question between the Apaches and the Government. For twenty years we have been held prisoners of war under a treaty that was made with General Miles. I think that my people are now capable of living in accordance with the laws of the United States and we would, of course, like to have the liberty to return to the land which is ours by divine right. Our people are decreasing in numbers here, and will continue to decrease unless they are allowed to return to their native land. Such a result is inevitable.

"There is no climate or soil which, to my mind, is equal to that of Arizona. It is my land, my home, my father's land, to which I now ask to be allowed to return. I want to spend my last days there, and be buried among those mountains. If this could be I might die in peace, feeling that my people, placed in their native homes, would increase in numbers, rather than diminish as at present, and that our name would not become extinct."

From the words of Goyahkla—Geronimo—as told to S. M. Barrett in 1906. Geronimo died and is buried in Oklahoma. In 1913, the Chiricahua were granted freedom, but not given their own lands.

In the 1970s, the U.S. government took away Western Apache cattle, claiming Apache herds were too large for the land they fed on. Partly as a result, some Apache Nations are worse off economically today than they were then.

In 1891, the Fort Apache Reservation was established, which has now been renamed the White Mountain Apache Nation. People on the San Carlos and White Mountain reservations began raising cattle in 1918, and soon after they began producing lumber. The Coolidge Dam brought many jobs for the Western Apaches, but after it was completed in the early 1930s, their farms were flooded out of existence. The government provided more cattle, but then took them away in the 1970s, claiming Apache lands were overgrazed.

Today, the White Mountain and San Carlos Apache each live on reservations named after their bands. The White Mountain Tribe is one of the largest Indian nations, with more than ten thousand members. San Carlos has over nine thousand. The Tonto Apache tribe has 132 members on their small reservation near Payson, Arizona. The Verde Valley Apache are politically paired with another tribe as the Yavapai-Apache Nation, yet they have kept their separate identity as Apache.

Over the past centuries, the diverse tribes of Apache Indians have survived wholesale slaughter, forced poverty, and blatant attempts to destroy their culture. Today's Apache nations are often combinations of groups

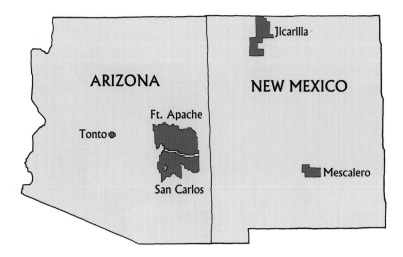

The dark portions of this map show the location of federally recognized Apache Tribes today. The Lipan Apache in Texas and Choctaw-Apache in Louisiana are still waiting to be formally recognized by the U.S. government.

who were historically different from one another. Some live far away from their homelands, others live on small portions of what used to be their grounds. Despite all these difficulties, the Apache today are proud people who enrich the world with their unique cultures.

In 1951, Wendell Chino was planning to serve his people on the Mescalero Apache Reservation as a Christian minister. Instead, he became one of the most influential Indian politicians of all time.

Chapter 3

Current Government

The American public may not know him as well as his forerunners Geronimo and *Cochise*, but Wendell Chino did more to impact the fortunes of American Indians than those legendary chiefs. Joann Mazzio summarized his life in an article for *Desert USA*.

Wendell Chino was born in 1924, the same year American Indians were first given the right to vote. His birthplace was the Mescalero Reservation in southern New Mexico. At that time, there were no industries on the reservation and few farms. The Mescalero Apache were mostly very poor. His parents, who had spent their childhood in captivity at Fort Sill, along with the entire Chiricahua tribe, had been freed only eleven years before Wendell's birth. They chose to move onto the Mescalero Reserve rather than continue struggling in Oklahoma.

As a young man, Wendell Chino did well in school. He went to a Christian college in Michigan, and returned to Mescalero with his degree and

Mescalero Apache tribal president Wendell Chino has been referred to as "the Father of Indian Casinos" because of his efforts to support tribal sovereignty and gaming rights.

license to be a minister. His calling turned out to be political, rather than spiritual, however.

Wendell Chino had a passionate desire to see his people move out of poverty. He wanted them to be modern, yet traditional as well. He said: "As the Apache people continue to adjust to a new culture, we hope that we can hold on to the best of the old—the wisdom and beauty of ancestral traditions."

When he was twenty-eight years old, Chino was elected to chair the Tribal Governing Committee, the most powerful political position in the tribe at that time. After that, the Mescalero Apache adopted a constitution with an elected president. Wendell Chino was elected the first president of the Mescalero Apache Nation.

The constitution calls for a presidential election every two years. A president can be reelected as many times as he or she chooses to run. Wendell Chino was reelected every other year, seventeen elections in a row. As chairman and then as president, he led the tribe for forty-three years.

Like everyone in politics, he had critics. But as he pointed out, "Wendell Chino doesn't elect himself. If the Apaches didn't like the way I was operating, they would have booted me out a long time ago." Wendell Chino led the Mescalero Nation out of poverty.

He was not a tall man, but he had a very powerful voice that he used to strongly express his views. Joann Mazzio writes: "His energy and iron will propelled his people into an economic growth never before experienced by other Native Americans." Under his leadership, a ski area was built on the Sierra Blanca Mountain; it is now the most popular ski slope in New Mexico. Lumber and manufacturing industries were started as well. A large hotel, the Inn of the Mountain Gods, attracted more tourists and brought more jobs for Apache people.

The Jicarilla tribal seal reflects their name, often interpreted as "little basket makers." It also displays the emblems of the two major clans, the Ollero and the Llanero. The economic roles of livestock and oil are also portrayed.

The key to Wendell Chino's success was his skill and persistence in talking to politicians outside of the reservation. As one reporter put it, "He set the standard for Indian *advocates* in the modern era of business suits and airline flights to Washington." He was well known at the New Mexico state government offices in Santa Fe, and in Washington, D.C. When the tribe was denied the right to serve alcohol at the Inn of the Mountain Gods, he took their case all the way to the U.S. Supreme Court. Someone said, "He's the E. F. Hutton of Indian Country—when he talks, people listen." Chino set an example of aggressive and intelligent political action that has been followed by many of today's Native politicians.

One of his most important contributions to modern America is Indian casino rights. The state of New Mexico opposed casinos, and Wendell Chino vigorously argued the right of Indian Nations to conduct gambling operations on their lands. Gaming has been called "the new buffalo," since it can potentially feed and house whole tribes, as the bison did in a less

Many new construction projects in the Jicarilla tribal lands—including a school, health center, and community center—reflect the successes of Jicarilla business and government leaders.

technical age. More than a hundred tribes now have casinos, due in part to Chino's strong efforts.

By the time he died in 1998, Wendell Chino had transformed the economic life of the Mescalero Reservation. The average income per person had increased three or four times from what it was before he took office. Real poverty had left the Nation. Chino liked to joke, "Zunis make jewelry, Navajos make rugs, Apaches make money." Chino did know how to make money, but he didn't do so for himself. He told a journalist: "Some tribal chairmen are not dedicated to their people. Instead of serving their people, they serve themselves." Wendell Chino served his people.

Indian tribes are regarded by the U.S. government as nations that have the right to elect their own governments, conduct their own businesses, and pass their own laws—providing these do not interfere with the Constitution of the United States. Since the Indian Reorganization Act of 1934, most tribes have adopted written constitutions, elected governments similar to that of the United States, and enrolled tribal members. All the Apache tribes follow this general pattern.

Tribal councils today have great power and responsibility in their communities. They protect the land and water rights of the tribe against outside interests. They negotiate with federal, state, and local governments, as well as with businesses and private parties. Tribal councils make laws for the tribe. They oversee land use. They watch over businesses and charitable organizations. In short, they are involved in almost every major matter within tribal borders.

The Apache today continue to produce strong, progressive leaders. Women have always played a strong role in social life, so it is not surprising that two tribes currently have women presidents. In Mescalero, Sara Misquez continues the pattern of solid business growth. In 2002, *The Almagordo Daily News* ran an article by Sandy Suggit about the opening of a new school. A U.S. senator told the crowd: "Your tribal council and president had to go out on a limb to get this building built."

The Mescalero Tribe is the only one who has built a school using only their own money to begin the work. In the end, the tribal council, tribal businesses, and promises from the government helped to see the school built. It cost $34 million and includes state-of-the-art computers and other facilities. A state school official said: "There's not any facility better in the nation." As important as the quality of the building is the style of education that will take place there. Both modern education and Mescalero Apache

Laurence Kie Jr. serves as conservation officer for the Jicarilla Apache Nation.

traditional ways will be taught. Students will be required to study their language. After the ribbon was cut, President Sara Misquez joined tribal dancers in celebration of the tribe's hopes for this school.

Under the leadership of tribal president Claudia Vigil-Muniz, elected in 2000, the Jicarilla Apache are also **optimistic** about new political developments. Claudia Vigil-Muniz is the mother of two grown children. She ran for president with vice presidential running mate Lamavaya Caramillo. Voters saw that the two would balance each other well; Vigil-Muniz has a degree from the college of Santa Fe, while Caramillo is perceived as somewhat more traditional, yet they work well together.

Claudia Vigil-Muniz comes from a family tradition of Jicarilla politics. Her father, Nossman Vigil, an artist, painted the Great Seal of the Jicarilla Apache Nation. Further back in family history, Augustin Vigil was one of six tribal leaders who traveled to Washington, D.C., in 1880. At that time, the tribe was in a difficult position without a reservation. As a result of the trip to D.C., the federal government agreed to give the Jicarilla their own lands, an important victory for the tribe.

Vigil-Muniz is the first woman president for the Jicarilla. A sign in her office says: "Women make great leaders: you're following one now." She is not trying to upset tradition, however, so she defers to the judgment of tribal elders and supports the continuation of the sacred rituals that have traditionally been only for men.

The San Carlos Apache Tribe also has a new tribal chairwoman. Kathleen Wesley Kitcheyan is the tribe's first chairwoman, having won the last election by a landslide. She has a master's degree in education and speaks fluent Chiricahua Apache. One tribal member describes her as "tough—and that's what we need." She also comes with a family tradition of leadership—Cochise was her ancestor.

Like the governments of all nations, Apache Nation governments must employ people to do office work, public utilities work, manage government resources, and enforce tribal laws. Laurence Kie Jr., for example, is a conservation officer for the Jicarilla Nation. He graduated from a police academy training course in Artesia, New Mexico, before starting the job, and now he works with eight full-time wardens to enforce the Jicarilla Nation Conservation Code. Most of Officer Kie's work is out in the field, where he covers 840,000 acres (approximately 340,200 hectares) of forested mountain, rugged *mesas*, and freshwater lakes. He usually works ten-hour shifts, but some days require twelve to sixteen hours of work. His duties are patroling, preventing crime, and keeping a high visibility. Some aspects of his job are pretty routine—such as enforcing litter laws. At other times, the job can get scary.

Poachers are a real problem. The Jicarilla Nation offers some of the world's best big game hunting and outstanding fishing. People try sneaking onto the land, rather than purchasing licenses. Officer Kie sees poaching as a sickness, like drug addiction—some people just have to keep doing it.

The tribe also has precious oil and gas resources, which people have tried to steal. An Indian Conservation Officer faces the same risks that all law enforcement officers encounter. Sometimes, people will pull guns. Officer Kie has to stay calm at all times and make quick decisions.

The Apache today are forging a new tradition of leadership: the tribal official. New leaders are as likely to be women as men. They are at home in the worlds of business and law. They can deal with big business and the needs of powerless individuals. Though they encounter a constantly changing world, they remain distinctly Apache.

Apache artist Duke Wasaaja Sine's interpretation of the origin of the traditional "crown dancers."

Chapter 4

Today's Spiritual Beliefs

Some American girls have special events to celebrate becoming women. A "sweet sixteen" birthday is supposed to be more special than most, and Hispanic girls look forward to their "quinciñera" at age fifteen. These celebrations are quite different, however, from the Sunrise Dance that marks an Apache girl's change from child to adult. Yes, she will receive gifts—but she will also receive a spiritual blessing, a challenge to her physical and emotional strength, and a powerful connection with the very beginning of Apache history.

This ceremony has various names. Since it commemorates physical changes from child to adult and takes place soon after a girl's first menstrual period, it is called the Puberty Ceremony. It is also called "the Changing Woman." (Changing Woman is the same person as White Painted Woman described in chapter one of this book.) The girl in the ceremony

Sine's image of Changing Woman.

becomes Changing Woman, who was the mother of all people and represents all the powers of women through the ages. In many accounts of the Creation, the rays of the Sun penetrate Changing Woman so she conceives the Monster Slayer; Rain then does the same, and she conceives the Child of Water. So the Sunrise Dance—performed while facing east—commemorates the sun bringing this change to Changing Woman/White Painted Woman. The White Mountain Apache name for this event is *Na-ih-es*.

For months before the ceremony, preparations are made. The girl's buckskin dress must be created. But she must not only look good on the outside—she also must be in good physical shape for the rigors of the ceremony. Plenty of food must be bought and prepared, because the family will be feeding participants and visitors. Since it costs thousands of dollars for the family to pay for the Sunrise Dance, extended family members usually help with expenses and preparations for the participants and visitors. Approximately one out of every three Apache young women have this experience, although the number is increasing. Sometimes the celebration is shortened to only one or two days from the usual four days, and sometimes several young women of the same age hold their ceremonies together.

A number of people have special roles in this ritual. A godmother is chosen for the girl, who will be a role model and have a special relationship with the girl throughout her life. A medicine person must oversee the entire ceremony and chant dozens of songs and prayers over the four days. Another young woman, often an older sister or cousin, assists the girl through the ceremony, dancing alongside her and supporting her if she grows weary. Among the Jicarilla, a young man participates in the Coming-of-Age Ceremony along with the young woman, symbolizing the importance of both male and female roles in nature.

During the ceremony, as the girl becomes Changing Woman, she acquires power to bless participants and bystanders. Traditionally, Changing Woman was washed ashore riding in a seashell, so the young woman wears a shell on her forehead. Throughout the four days, she must remain painted with a sacred mixture of cornmeal and clay. She can only scratch with a sacred stick when it itches, and she can only drink with a special straw out of a ceremonial cup. Since she becomes White Painted Woman, she must also act like a supernatural being. Throughout four days of songs, prayers, and dances, she must do everything right. She must not be cross, even though she will be tired and uncomfortable. She must perform all her actions in the ritual flawlessly.

At night, the Gaan visit her. These are called by different names; Crown Dancers describes their attire. Prejudiced people trying to discredit the Apache culture called them Devil Dancers, although they do not represent evil. A more accurate description would be "mountain spirits." These masked and painted dancers represent powerful supernatural ancestral beings who come to purify and bless the girl and other participants in the ceremony.

On the last day of the dance, the girl blesses all that are attending the event. Those who are sick receive healing from her touch. She also receives gifts from those who have come.

The Sunrise Dance fulfills a number of important functions. Young women who have done this speak about how it gave them a new sense of spiritual power and inner goodness. It also gives them a strong public identity as an Apache woman. It binds the community together, as they share an experience of worship while praying and giving and receiving gifts. Finally, it keeps the whole community firmly connected to their spiritual beliefs and roots as a people.

A variety of other traditional ceremonies are also practiced in the Apache nations. Most of these ceremonies are closed to non-Apache, and there's a good reason for this. Older men and women recall a time not so long ago when they were punished for any expression of their traditional beliefs. They have experienced white people seeking to learn their spiritual ways—only to later mock or punish those ways. Other people have imitated their dances and prayers, but they have not done so properly. It takes years and years of *apprenticeship* to become a medicine person. Spiritual

The Gaan, or Mountain Spirit Dancers, represent powerful supernatural ancestral beings, who come to purify and bless the girl and other participants in the Changing Woman ceremony.

The Apache and other native cultures regard certain mountains and other natural sites as sacred. The development of an observatory atop Mount Graham in Arizona has upset many traditional Apache, who revere the site as a sacred altar.

power is a tricky thing, sort of like taking physical medicine. The same elements can heal or cause damage. If people perform Apache rituals the wrong way, harm might result.

On some Apache reservations, the old beliefs and ceremonies may be in danger of being lost. Among the Jicarilla, for instance, it has been hard to find young men willing to make the financial and time sacrifices required to learn the ways of the medicine men. There used to be one man who knew all the words to an important ceremonial dance; now three men have to do it because there isn't one man who knows all the words. If younger people don't learn these sacred ways, the dance may disappear in coming decades.

One issue for traditional Apache is the observatory on Mount Graham.

This mountain is adjacent to the San Carlos Reservation, and it is the home of the Gaan and a sacred Apache altar. It is also an unusually fine place to construct a giant telescope, enabling astronomers to peer far into space. The University of Arizona and the **Vatican** together developed the observatory—but it has disturbed the San Carlos Apache's personal prayers and observances. Furthermore, the Apache believe that the mountain itself is a living being who is being damaged. Apache, environmentalists, politicians, and artists have joined together to protest the use of the observatory on Mount Graham. Not all the San Carlos Apache agree on this issue, though. Sacred beliefs differ between Apache people, and some believe that the impoverished San Carlos Reservation would benefit from the jobs brought by a large development project close to their homes.

Although ceremonies play a part in traditional Apache religion, Apache belief is more wide ranging, not limited to only special days and places. For

Saint Joseph's Catholic Church was founded at Mescalero in 1887. In 1917, Geronimo's son Robert was married in this church. Most of the Christians in Mescalero are either Catholic or Reformed.

Bik'egu´indá´n

This icon by artist Robert Lentz portrays Christ as a Mescalero Holy Man. It serves as the Crucifix at St. Joseph's Catholic Church on the Mescalero Apache Reservation in New Mexico.

both young and old Apache, their spiritual life is something they practice every day, wherever they are. They contrast their spirituality with the way they see Christianity. From their perspective, Christianity appears to be a "Sunday religion," a spirituality confined to a narrow place and time.

A significant number of Apache belong to the Native American Church. This form of worship combines Christian beliefs with an emphasis on Indian pride, strong morals, and traditional ceremonies. The movement began among the Kiowa and Apache in Oklahoma around 1890. In 1918, followers from a number of tribes incorporated their movement as the Native American Church. It is a "Pan-Indian" belief, not belonging to any one tribe but uniting the faith of diverse Native peoples. The Native American Church claims 250,000 members in the United States, Mexico, and Canada.

Many Apaches are also committed to the Christian faith—either Catholic or Protestant. It is hard to estimate how many follow the old ways or how many identify themselves as Christians. People on the same reservation

Robert Soto performs a hoop dance before an appreciative audience. Soto is a Lipan Apache living in Texas. He and his family use traditional dances to share their culture and to communicate the Gospel message. Robert is part of a growing movement of Native people who worship Christ using traditional American Indian music and dances.

This painting by Duke Wasaaja Sine is titled Blessings of the Gahn.

have different opinions. One says, "Most people are traditional in their beliefs here," and the next one claims, "Seventy percent of the reservation are Christian." Some people share their allegiance between Christian faith and traditional beliefs, while others feel they cannot be mixed. Roman Catholics tend to believe that Native religion can be combined with Christian beliefs, rites, and sacraments, while Pentecostals are more likely to make a clean break from their tradition to embrace the new faith.

Pentecostal churches emphasize the Bible as God's literal written word. Pentecostal worship focuses on direct experience of God's Spirit. Worshipers may speak in "tongues"—*ecstatic* utterances that resemble foreign languages. Services are emotional and lively. *Evangelical* and Pentecostal churches emphasize the need for people to have personal relationships

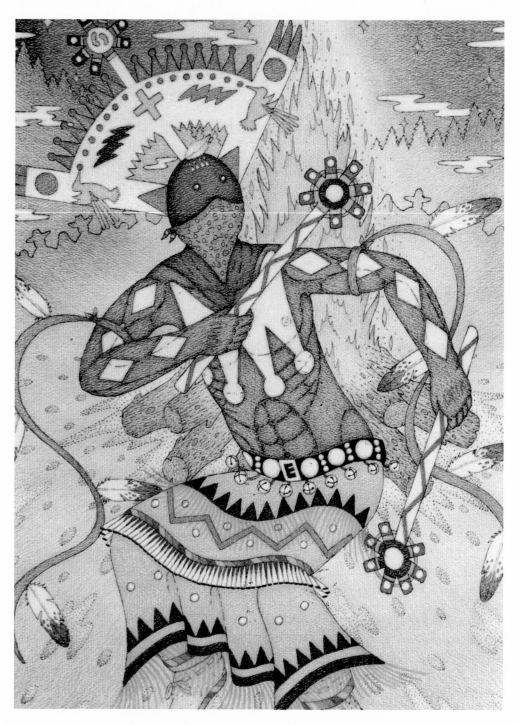

Apache Gahn Dancer *by Duke Wasaaja Sine.*

with Christ. They emphasize the power of such conversions to change lives and overcome destructive habits. Drinking and smoking are discouraged.

Soon after the Chiricahua were imprisoned at Fort Sill, the Reformed Church of America established a church there to care for the spiritual and physical needs of the Apache. Geronimo wrote in his autobiography: "I have adopted the Christian religion. I believe that the church has helped me much during the short time I have been a member." Today, there are Apache Reformed Churches in Oklahoma and at Mescalero. At the Mescalero Reformed Church, each service includes a prayer said in Apache by a member of the congregation, and hymns and praise songs sung in Apache. The sermon is in English. They have an active youth group that meets together for fun and spiritual support.

Saint Joseph's Catholic Church was founded at Mescalero in 1887. In 1917, Geronimo's son Robert was married in the church. The altar of the church is an *icon* called *The Apache Christ*, portraying Jesus as a Mescalero medicine person. Most of the Christians in Mescalero are either Catholic or Reformed. Many people would say they are both Christian and traditional.

The San Carlos Reservation is peppered with Christian churches of every sort—Baptists, Charismatics, Pentecostals, Lutherans, Mormons, and so on. Many of these churches are small and meet in people's homes. The majority is Pentecostal.

Whether they pray with cornmeal and tobacco, or with a priest in church, Apache find comfort and strength in their spiritual beliefs. Some reservations have high unemployment, and teens face problems not unlike those in inner-city America. Spiritual beliefs help the Apache cope with these pressures. Yet, some Apache are spiritually searching—unsure what they believe. As one esteemed medicine man told me, "Some are Christian, and some are Traditional, yet there are many who are lost."

Many Apache social structures are built on the Apache's sense of connection to one another and to the natural world.

Chapter 5

Social Structures Today

You probably have a favorite radio station. Most people like stations that play their favorite music or have their favorite personalities. Radio station KNNB on the White Mountain Apache Reservation, however, is more than popular—people's lives can depend on its broadcasting.

KNNB is 88.1 on the FM dial. Local people refer to it as "Apache Radio." The announcers do their shows both in Apache and in English. Programming varies from parenting tips to health advice to a broad variety of music—*reggae*, country, rock, and gospel. The station has remarkable success in reaching its audience—97 percent of White Mountain's population listens to it.

KNNB has a role much more vital than entertainment or giving tips: it is a valuable tool for communicating public safety messages. Forty percent of the households on the reservation lack telephones, so the station may be the only way for people to get urgent messages. If someone is missing or in trouble, that information is broadcast over the radio so help can be given.

In June 2002, the terrible Chediski-Rodeo wildfire swept through eastern Arizona. It destroyed hundreds of homes and burned half a million acres (approximately 202,500 hectares) of the Fort Apache Reservation. In this frightening time, KNNB was a lifeline. Volunteers helped the station stay constantly on the air. They told people where they had to evacuate and where help was needed to relieve people who had to move. At 630 watts, KNNB is a relatively small broadcaster, but the station is hugely important to the White Mountain Apache community.

Of course, not all Apache today live on the reservation. In chapter seven you'll meet some tribal members who have pursued careers outside their Apache Nation lands. When thinking about social structures and Native American people today, one Native man refers to "Urban Indians," "At-Home Indians," and "In-and-Out Indians."

The first expression is obvious: "Urban Indians" are those who live in the big cities like New York, home to 87,000 Native people, and Los Angeles, home to 53,000. Only one reservation in America has a Native population larger than these cities. The expression "At-Home Indians" reflects the fact that great numbers of *indigenous* people in North America still live on their tribal reservation, and many who live elsewhere still consider tribal lands to be "home." (Of course, there are also many "Urban Indians" who now consider home to be the community where they have settled.) "In-and-Out Indians" are those whose lives bring them back to tribal lands for a while, then take them back to the cities.

Many Native people would be hard to fit neatly into one of these categories. This is an area where stereotypes can happen very easily. Even among Indians, stereotypes become associated with people based on where they live, rather than who they are.

While some Apache live off the reservation, many still make their homes there. A sense of comfort comes from the closeness of family and community cultural traditions. A man in San Carlos explained a practical reason for living on the reservation: "Life here is better than off reservation because you don't need a lot of money. In Phoenix, I'd go broke in a day."

Women continue to have a strong role in Apache communities. Historically, women made many of the practical day-to-day decisions for families, and they also fulfilled most family responsibilities. As Stephen Trimble

A Jicarilla Apache family's artistic heritage can be seen in this picture. From left to right, Grandma Thelma Velarde, who practiced the traditional art of Jicarilla pottery making, and cousins Sheldon Nunez-Velarde, potter, and Ollie Velarde, painter. Families are very important to Apache cultures today.

writes in his book, *The People*: "They are the trunk of the family tree, their children its branches, their husbands sometimes described as leaves. The Apache say: 'The leaves may drop off, but the trunk and the branches never break.'" Among the Jicarilla, women own cattle, horses, and homes.

Apache are giving people—especially when it comes to family. Some twenty-first-century social forces can harm families in today's Apache society, but members of the extended family can still always be counted on to help. If someone loses a job and needs a home, or if divorce or other

Apache lands in New Mexico and Arizona are arid and forested, which makes it very easy for fires to start and burn out of control.

problems cause a wife or child to move out, members of the extended family will always take them in.

An important aspect of Apache culture is the clan. Clans are groups of families related through a common female ancestor. Dale Curtis Miles (San Carlos Apache) writes: "Our elaborate clan system extends through all the Western Apache country. Clan—traced through a person's mother—is considered a blood relationship, so a person can claim a connection to a band a hundred miles away." The Mescalero, San Carlos, and White Mountain Apache have **matriarchal** clans, so marriage within one's clan is strictly forbidden.

The Jicarilla have always had a different sort of clan system from that of the Western Apaches. Jicarilla clans are more of a political system. The entire Nation is divided into just two clans—the two historical bands, Ollero and Llanero. The clan's strength relies on numbers, so Jicarilla clans are the opposite from other Apache groups, marriages within the clan are actually encouraged.

Women have historically made many of the day-to-day decisions for Apache families, and they continue to have a strong role in Apache communities. This clan mother of a century ago would be able to relate to the important cultural role of her great-granddaughters today.

Ever since the Spanish brought horses to the New World, the Apache cultures have shown wonderful skills in riding and great love for their steeds. Among the Apaches today there are outstanding rodeo performers. Many Apache families enjoy having horses.

The Lipan Apache also identify strongly with bands. Relocating among the Kickapoo in Mexico, and then moving back into Texas, they have moved together as bands. Recently, they have begun to form some identity as a tribe in the hope of gaining government recognition, but they still feel strongest allegiance to their bands.

Sports are important among all the Apache tribes. On the White Mountain Reservation, basketball is very popular. Basketball great Kareem Abdul-Jabbar spent a season there coaching the Alchesay High School Falcons. Abdul-Jabbar wrote about his experiences coaching at White Mountain in his book, *A Season on the Reservation*. He tells how his time with the

Falcons rekindled his love for basketball. He was impressed with the speed of the team: "These kids went from zero to full speed in almost nothing flat. They had only one gear—all out."

The Mescalero Reservation is further south, closer to Texas where everyone seems to love football. That may be why football rather than basketball reigns supreme in the Mescalero Apache Nation. Whatever their favorite sport, however, all Apache are enthusiastic fans of their local teams.

Centuries of hostility from European cultures have had a negative impact on the life patterns of the various Apache tribes. Attempts to wipe out whole bands or tribes, diseases, deliberately imposed poverty, and starvation have severely tested the strengths of Native cultures. In the minds of some Apache, the most damaging assaults were the nineteenth-century attempts to erase their culture. Government schools severely punished children for speaking their own language or keeping their customs, and ceremonial aspects of traditional religious life were not allowed on the reservations. One indian agent at the Mescalero reservation was so incredibly out of touch with the people there that he prohibited the Sunrise Dance, believing this celebration of womanhood was an auctioning off of young women.

A San Carlos member privately lamented the loss of some traditional family ways. Children don't learn from their parents and elders the way they used to, he complained. They aren't encouraged enough to speak Apache at home. *HUD housing* has broken up clans, so clan customs break down. "Today, not many people are living the traditional way anymore," he concludes sadly. A major reason for these problems is that "the older people weren't allowed to live their lives" in accordance with their beliefs.

Because of the loss of traditional ways, and the loss of identity that follows, unhealthy social patterns such as alcohol abuse, drug abuse, violence, and crime have had a tragic impact on some Apache nations. Poverty and unemployment sometimes add to these unfortunate trends. Native people in the Phoenix, Arizona, health care region have the highest homicide death rate in the country—20.7 violent deaths per 100,000 people. Alcohol is often a problem associated with violence. One young man, who pleaded guilty to shooting another tribal member on the White Mountain Reservation, said: "Alcohol has been a problem for my family for as long as I can remember." Suicide is also alarmingly high on some Apache reservations.

Of course, none of these problems are unique to the Apache people—

Most Apache today live in frame houses or manufactured homes, though some live in clustered HUD housing.

or to Native Americans. Prejudice, poverty, and government dependency challenge many people of all races throughout America. One factor that has made things especially difficult for some Apache tribes, however, is the geographic location of their reservations. Lack of access to major cities has hindered attempts to strengthen the local economy.

One important event, which keeps traditional cultural ways strong among the Jicarilla, is the Go-Jii-Ya feast, the Jicarilla version of the Thanksgiving holiday. It is celebrated September 14 through 15, at Stone Lake, on the Jicarilla Reservation. This celebration originated hundreds of years ago when the two clans of the Jicarilla—the Ollero and Llanero—lived as separate bands. Whenever they happened to meet, the Go-Jii-Ya was celebrated. In the late 1800s, when the Jicarilla were moved onto the reservation, this became a set date. Families build brush arbors to cook in, and they sleep out in tepees; they live in ways the Jicarilla lived in centuries past. A great amount of food is cooked. One of the more exotic dishes is buffalo-crawfish *jambalaya*. The two clans compete in foot races.

Broad generalizations can't be made about social structures among the Apache Indians today. Some people live in large cities, others on tribal reservations. Many live on reservations that belong to other tribes. Traditions vary between the different Apache nations. Each person, in his or her own way, strives to retain a unique Apache identity while living successfully in today's world.

This bronze sculpture, titled Lament, *by Allan Houser, is part of the Allan Houser Sculpture Garden located on the 110-acre (44.6-hectare) Allan Houser Compound in Santa Fe, New Mexico. Allan Houser was very proud of his Chiricahua Apache heritage, which is reflected in the many artistic mediums with which he worked.*

Chapter 6

Contemporary Arts

He was the first child of his nation born free from government imprisonment. By the time he died, he had been recognized by a U.S. president and given every award the art world could offer. When Allan Houser, Chiricahua Apache, left this world in 1994, he was recognized as one of the most important artists of the twentieth century.

Allan's father, Sam Haozous, was among those jailed at Castillo De San Marcos in St. Augustine, Florida, after Geronimo's surrender. Allan's father served as an interpreter for that famous chief. Allan's mother, Blossom, was born in a prison camp at Mount Vernon Barracks, Alabama. His parents met and married at Fort Sill, Oklahoma, where the Chiricahua were kept captive until 1913. Their family name, "Haozous," means "pulling up roots out of the ground," which refers to the practice of giving thanks to the earth whenever people take something from her.

The Chiricahua were officially released from captivity shortly before Allan's birth. The majority of the Chiricahua Nation moved north to live with

By the time he died in 1994, Chiricahua Apache artist Allan Houser had won almost every major art award.

the Mescalero in New Mexico. Sam and Blossom Haozous remained in Oklahoma, where Allan grew up on a farm, helping his parents raise cotton, alfalfa, livestock, and horses.

When Allan was a child, pictures in books and magazines fascinated him. He made drawings based on stories his father told him about battles, buffalo hunts, and life when the Apache lived freely, and from his mother's songs about love for her children. He said in a 1990 interview: "My mother and father made me proud of who I am. I was always proud of them and the hardships they went through. I'm always telling kids, you've got to feel good about yourself. I'm saying, this is the way we look. Look at the beauty."

In 1934, Allan enrolled for art lessons at the Santa Fe Indian School, also known as the Dorothy Dunn School. Allan Houser became the school's most famous student. By 1939, his art was exhibited in San Francisco, Washington, D.C., and Chicago. That same year, he married Anna Marie Gallegos. In 1941, they moved with their three young sons to Los Angeles,

California. There he became familiar with modern European artists who inspired his later artistic achievements.

In 1947, the Haskell Institute in Lawrence, Kansas, commissioned Allan to do a memorial sculpture to honor Indian students from Haskell who died in World War II. This work was called *Comrade in Mourning*. It was his first major marble carving.

Four years later Allan moved to Brigham City, Utah. For the next eleven years he taught art at the Inter-Mountain Indian School. In 1954, the French government honored him with the Palmes d'Acadamique for his outstanding achievement as a teacher and artist.

Allan Houser was invited to join the newly created Institute of American Indian Arts in Santa Fe, New Mexico in 1962. He created the department of sculpture there. His approach to sculpture, which combined North American Indian traditional themes with modernist styles, influenced hundreds of other artists and earned worldwide recognition.

In 1975, Houser retired from teaching in order to devote his energy to his own art. Over the next nineteen years, he produced a thousand sculptures in stone, wood, and bronze. His works have been displayed in Europe and Asia, and he received practically every award the art world can bestow.

In 1992, President George Bush Sr. awarded Allan Houser with the National Medal of Arts. Houser was the first Native American Indian to receive the country's highest artistic honor. As he presented the award, President Bush said: "His hands transform bronze and stone to capture the true meaning of this country's unbroken spirit. His sculptures eloquently echo this nation's heritage of proud Apache chiefs and speak for the essential humanity of all Americans." Allan Houser died on August 22, 1994, leaving a legacy of profound influence on the art world.

Bob Haozous, the son of Allan and Ann Houser, is also a noted artist. He is a member of the Warm Springs Chiricahua Apache Tribe of Oklahoma, located in Apache, Oklahoma. He produces works in a variety of *organic* and *synthetic mediums*. His art causes the viewer to take a look—sometimes an uncomfortable look—at serious issues like sexual exploitation, genocide, and warfare.

His work has been described as "a combination of biting humor and direct honesty." He asks:

Where in our arts do we see statements that bring the serious issues of alcoholism, suicide, *diabetes*, poverty, ignorance, early death, land loss, environmental destruction, and the general loss of all *aboriginal* cultures? If these issues are truly serious, where is the internal cultural dialogue, and to whom does the artist target this dialogue, and just what is the role of the Native American artist? . . . As native people our true value is not in worshipping what was, but to use history as one of many references to create a new dialogue that helps determine what should be.

Another noted Apache artist today is Duke Wsaaja Sine. He is half Yavapai, half San Carlos Apache. His father, David V. Sine, is also an artist. Duke Sine using watercolors or mixed mediums on paper. He received training in the basics of art from his father and then earned a formal art degree from the Institute of American Indian Arts in Santa Fe. His works are in galleries and art museums throughout the southwestern United States. He says, "My paintings are not just pretty pictures, but each one has its own story. My style has developed from a respect for traditional Indian art as well as a vision toward the future of Indian art."

Duke Wasaaja Sine is another Apache artist. He created this pen and ink and watercolor drawing titled Guardians of the Apache.

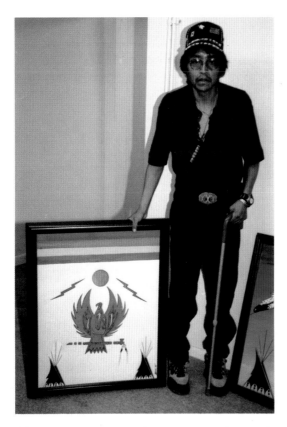

Oley Velarde and his paintings. His works are composed around Jicarilla traditional symbols and designs.

The vitality of Apache art is evident at the Jicarilla Apache Cultural Center in Dulce, New Mexico. Visitors there can see a number of artists working at a large table. Ollin "Oley" Velarde, for example, is an acrylic painter. He began painting at Mountainview High School in Utah, but then went to the Institute of American Indian Arts in Santa Fe. His paintings combine bright colors and traditional Apache designs. One of his paintings represents the two Jicarilla clans, the Ollero and Llanero, with their banners and tepees.

Rowyn H. Elote is Oley's cousin. He is a man of many talents: he has won prizes in the rodeo, including at the 2000 National Rodeo Finals. He serves as a hunting guide, runs landscaping machinery, and produces art in chalk, pastel, and acrylics. He doesn't do any preliminary outlines with pencil, like most artist—just moves his pen quickly. The result may be a

Jicarilla Apache artist Oley Velarde shows an acrylic painting he is working on.

beautiful lifelike elk or some other object from nature. Both Rowyn and Ollin are ambidextrous—they can produce amazing pictures with either hand!

Sheldon Nunez-Velarde is another member of this talented family, an artist who produces micaceous pottery. Mica is a mineral that is found in thin, brittle sheets in the ground. It looks almost like glass. When broken up in clay, mica produces pottery that shines in the sun like gold. There is a story—no one knows if it is true—that the Spanish *conquistadors* heard about "cities of gold" in New Mexico because they mistook micaceous pottery for gold. Whether or not the story is true, the Ollero clan of the Jicarilla was making micaceous pottery before Columbus came to the New World. Pottery served *utilitarian* functions for holding water, cooking, and food storage. The Jicarillas also bartered their pottery to neighboring tribes, and later to their Spanish neighbors.

Sheldon is imposing in stature, but his friendly personality and sense of humor soon put guests at ease. He makes pottery in his home. Pottery making has been done in the family for four generations, starting with his great, great, great-grandmother, O'ha Montoya. Her earlier works inspire many of the traditional Apache shapes and designs in Sheldon Nunez-Velarde's pottery.

Rowyn Elote is a man of many talents: rodeo rider, hunting guide, and artist.

Sheldon Nunez-Velarde's pottery is made of glittering micaceous clay, a beautiful art form practiced by the Ollero Clan of the Jicarillas for untold centuries. The Spanish name, "Ollero" means "potters."

The first step in making micaceous pottery is to gather the raw materials. Sheldon travels three hours east of his home in Dulce to dig the clay in lands once owned by his Jicarilla ancestors. Like other Indian potters, he shows respect for Mother Earth by praying and making offerings before gathering clay. He takes only what is needed.

The clay must then be soaked in water for several days and sifted to remove chunks of foreign material. It is then put into cotton sacks and placed in the sun so the water in it will evaporate. Next, the clay is kneaded to eliminate air bubbles. Bubbles in the clay could cause pottery to explode during firing. Sheldon Nunez-Velarde then forms the pot by hand, coiling the clay in a long snake he shapes into a circle. Once the pot is shaped, it is left to dry for three or four days until it becomes leather hard. It is then sanded with sandstone, found in the surrounding mountains. The surface is polished with a crystal rock.

Finally, the pot is ready to be fired. It is placed inside an oven and slowly baked until the oven has reached its highest temperature. In the meantime, a fire has been started outside from oak wood, which makes hot coals. The

Shiny mica mixed into the clay gives it a beautiful golden glitter when finished.

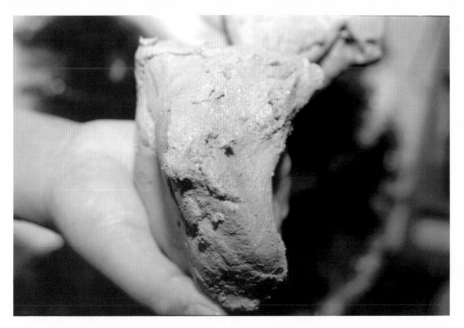

Sheldon gathers clay three hours from his home, in land that used to be Jicarilla country. He prays and makes offerings before taking the clay.

After a piece of pottery is formed, it is dried until it becomes leather hard before polishing and firing.

Burden baskets were practical, unbreakable containers used by nomadic bands.

pot is covered with wood and the fire fully hardens the clay. This is a very tricky process, and much experience is needed to do it well.

Once the pots are removed and cooled, Sheldon examines the results of his labors. He is happy to see, "a gleaming natural gold-flaked sheen." This means "the hard work has paid off."

Basket weaving is another traditional art form for which the Apaches are famous. "Burden baskets" were practical containers for the ***nomadic*** bands to carry in ancient days, used to carry wood and harvested crops. Baskets were used as cooking pots, water jugs, and serving platters. Today, burden baskets are used for traditional ceremonies and for sale. The size of the basket indicates its purpose: the smallest are medicine baskets, and medium-sized wedding baskets are for gifts and weddings. The largest are burden baskets and bread baskets.

Burden baskets are woven from strips of cottonwood, willow, mulberry, and devil's claw bush. After weaving, they are decorated with tassels and jingles. The tassels, made of deer or cow skin, are both ceremonial and decorative. Two stories are told about the jingles. One story says they were first invented to keep snakes away while gathering food. Another story is connected to the custom that Apache sons-in-law should never be in the presence of their mothers-in-law. The jingles served as a warning of approaching mothers-in-law. Whatever the real reason for them, the tassels and jingles make Apache burden baskets both beautiful and melodious.

The art of basket weaving has been passed down from grandmother to mother to daughter, for generations. There are not as many basket

A tightly woven grass basket made by the San Carlos Apache is on display at the San Carlos Apache Cultural Center.

weavers today as there used to be, however, for it is a very time-consuming craft. An Apache burden basket is truly a treasure for its owner.

American Indian artists have lost great amounts of money in recent years due to fake "Indian" art produced in Asian factories. Millions of dollars in sales have been stolen from Native Americans this way. The best way to make sure something is genuine is to buy from the artist who makes it, or from Reservation Cultural Centers who will only deal with tribal members.

Some people think genuine American Indian art is expensive, but they are not aware of the many hours it takes to create handmade art. When you take the artists' time into consideration, it is obvious Native artists sell their crafts for very reasonable amounts. Art sales are important means of income for many Indians today. When you buy their crafts, you are getting

Seed beads woven onto a loom are another form of Jicarilla Apache artwork.

Franklin Stanley Sr. meticulously threads seed beads. He is a Chiricahua Apache enrolled as San Carlos. He does whole pieces of beaded art without sketching out the design. His work is a reminder of his words, that fine handmade art cannot be produced "by the truckload."

more than an object—you are getting an expression of the life and heritage of the maker.

As Franklin Stanley Sr., a member of the San Carlos Apache tribe, sat meticulously threading tiny seed beads to create an intricate design, he said: "Native American people will make things, but not by the truckload." Objects of true beauty are not mass-produced.

Earl Sisto, a Yavapai-Apache living in Southern California, is director of the Native American Student Programs at the University of California, Riverside. Here he is dressed in powwow attire.

Chapter 7

Contributions to the World

Earl Sisto is a Yavapai-Apache, who began life on the San Carlos Reservation and now lives in Southern California. He has benefited greatly from the Indian relocation program, which the government sponsored in the 1950s and 1960s. This program provided help with job training and housing for Indians who left the reservations for economic opportunities offered in the cities. Around 160,000 Native people participated in the program.

Some have criticized the relocation program as harming the reservations, but others point to the opportunities it has given participants. Earl Sisto contributes much to Indians throughout the country, and he has a strong sense of his Apache identity, even though he resides in California.

He was born in San Carlos, Arizona. As a child, he lived in a *wickiup*—the traditional housing for some of the Apache tribes. He learned how to tolerate cold weather in winter. In the summer, with little to drink, he tracked down horses in the hot desert. During the school year he attended a federal government school on the reservation. There he earned perfect attendance awards for six years in a row. When he was in seventh grade, something happened that shows why many Indians are bitter when they recall government schooling. A white teacher literally tried to choke Earl Sisto to death for saying a few words in the Apache language.

Following graduation, he enrolled in Phoenix, Arizona, Junior College. Then in 1964, he moved to Los Angeles through the relocation program. He worked for a telephone company during the next decade and also pursued more education. He earned a bachelor's degree in 1974 in fine arts from the University of California–Los Angeles. He then worked as a community representative for the Indian Education Program in the Los Angeles public school district. In 1991, he took his present position as director of Native American Student Programs at the University of California, Riverside. He remains connected to life at San Carlos Reservation, going back on regular visits and participating in the life of the community when he can be helpful.

One of the Apache's greatest contributions to our world is their sense of the importance of harmony with nature. Our earth's future health may depend on our ability to hear the message of Native thinkers.

Amaurante Montez is of Apache/Yaqui/Aztec background. He produces "postmodern urban tribal" music for raves, hip-hop shows, and DJ battles. He owns his own multimedia production company: Mayaglyph Inc. He also does storytelling and plays the traditional American Indian wooden flute. Amaurante calls his flute "the lady who travels with me."

He has been able to help many young Native people around the country get into college and achieve academic success.

Like many Native people today, Earl Sisto is active in artistic and cultural endeavors. He has participated in art shows and won awards. He also does **powwow** dancing and has won awards for that. He has even been part of powwows in Hawaii and Athens, Greece. He also traveled to Japan to demonstrate American Indian dances.

The Apache nations contribute significantly to the lives of both Native and non-Native Americans. Wendell Chino, who was discussed in chapter three, was a role model for Indian leaders across America. His style of firm political pressure was a successful strategy for advancing North American Indian rights in America. Allan Houser was one of the monumental figures in the world art scene throughout past decades. His work influenced Indian and non-Indian artists in America and in Europe.

Today, Mary Kim Titla, San Carlos Apache (see cover), is a general assignment reporter for Arizona's KPNX Channel 12 news. She received her bachelor's degree in journalism from the University of Oklahoma and a master's degree in mass communication from Arizona State University. She has received numerous awards for her reporting, including first-place awards from the Associated Press, Arizona Press Club, and Native American Journalists Association. Outstanding Young Women of America and the YWCA have also recognized her. She received the Ira Hayes Honorable Warrior award for her work with Native American Youth in 2002. That award is named after the Pima soldier who raised the flag at Iwa Jima during World War II.

As a television anchor in Phoenix, Arizona, she has helped non-Native people to understand more about their Indian neighbors. She says: "Arizonians have been around Indians all their lives; they should already know each tribe has its own culture and language. But media haven't always paid attention. Too often media only cover the negative aspects of minority cultures." Mary Kim Titla and other minority broadcasters are playing a key role in overcoming such problems. Titla affirms: "If we all knew more about each other, what a better place the world would be."

Raoul Trujillo is another face becoming more familiar to American audi-

Raoul Trujillo, of Apache/Ute/Mexican and French-Canadian ancestry, is a dancer, choreographer, and actor on stage, television, and in the movies.

ences. A dancer, **choreographer**, and actor, he is of Apache/Ute/Mexican and French-Canadian ancestry. He wrote and directed the musical *Tribe* at the Ordway Center for Performing Arts in St. Paul, Minnesota, and a mythological **cabaret**, *FORBIDDEN GODdeSses*, with Native Earth Performing Arts and Buddies and Bad Times Theatre in Toronto, Canada. On television he has appeared on *La Femme Nikita*, *Divided Loyalties*, *Jag*, and *Lonesome Dove*. Movie appearances include *Black Robe*, *Shadow of the Wolf*, and *Highlander III*.

Contemporary Apache like Trujillo, Titla, and Sisto have given much both to their own people and to the world in general. But it is not just the outstanding figures who have made important contributions. The Apache people's culture, courage, and rich artistic heritage all enrich our world.

As the Apache move into the twenty-first century, their sense of relationship with the earth will play a role in their future. This picture, Speaking Back to the Night, *by Apache artist Sine, portrays the communion that many Apaches feel with the natural world.*

Chapter 8

Challenges for Today, Hopes for the Future

Stacey Sanchez has good reasons to be upbeat. She is the tribal public relations person for the Jicarilla Apache Nation. Even a casual observer can see good things happening around Dulce, Arizona, the heart of Jicarilla lands. At the Best Western motel, a business owned and operated by the Jicarilla, rooms are sold out months in advance by sportsmen, tourists, and construction workers. Just up the street from the motel, a new sports complex is being constructed. A little ways south from there, a large elementary school building is being constructed. Across the street, a new hospital is also rising from the ground. Along with all this, a new wastewater treatment facility and new justice center complex are in construction. In December 2002, a new shopping center and new housing complex were completed. Just driving around Jicarilla, visitors can plainly see that this is a community "on the go."

Stacey Sanchez is the tribal public relations director for the Jicarilla Apache Nation.

Economic development is important for all Indian nations. A history of oppressive or ineffective U.S. federal policies has left many tribes struggling financially. The Jicarilla are fortunate in terms of natural resources and outstanding tribal leadership. Oil and gas on Jicarilla lands enabled them to sign profitable leases in the 1970s and '80s. In 1996, the Jicarilla

Oil and gas on Jicarilla lands enabled the tribe to sign profitable leases in the 1970s and 1980s. The tribe invested income from these resources carefully, enabling them to plan for a prosperous future.

The Jicarilla Reservation covers 840,000 acres (approximately 340,200 hectares) of scenic mountains, rugged mesas, and fresh lakes and streams.

signed the largest Indian water rights settlement in the United States—26 million dollars. New Mexico faces a water shortage, so the Jicarilla, whose lands are on the watershed divide, are in a good place.

The Jicarilla have made decisions that have greatly multiplied the benefits of good fortune. They carefully chose investment consultants and invested their monies to make more. Dividends off these investments have been distributed to tribal members. The tribe also set up a scholarship fund, knowing that education is key for the future. As a result of these efforts, the Jicarilla Nation had only a 17 percent unemployment rate at the end of 2002. This is very healthy, compared to most Indian tribes in North America. Three out of four Jicarilla high school students graduate, which is also a very positive statistic.

The Jicarilla Fish and Game Department plays a crucial role in tribal life. Since tribal lands extend seventy miles (approximately 119 kilometers) north and south, it can take more than two hours to reach some parts of the reservation using 4x4 trucks. It is a sportsman's or nature lover's paradise. Mountains are covered with pines, and streams and lakes nestle in the valleys. More than five thousand mule deer and four thousand elk make their homes on the reserve, as do black bears, turkeys, mountain lions, and rainbow trout.

The Jicarilla Fish and Game Department cares for invaluable natural resources. The Jicarilla Apache Nation in northern New Mexico is a sportsman's paradise.

Eudané Vicenté loves working for the Fish and Game Department. His job means he spends most of his time in the outdoors. He says: "Most people don't get to see critters like this—they have to pay people like me to see them." The rangers of the Fish and Game Department are responsible for managing fish and wildlife populations and habitats. They have to gather great amounts of information on the animals and plant life throughout Jicarilla lands. They set quotas and dates for hunting and fishing seasons, make sure people have the right licenses, and so on. Judging from sportsmen's trophy kills, Jicarilla has the best mule deer hunting in North America. They are also noted for elk hunting.

Sportsmen come to hunt Jicarilla game from all over the world. These are "quality not quantity" hunts. An elk permit costs $4,500 to $6,000. A mule deer permit costs $10,000. No more than twenty sportsmen at a time are granted permits, and they are spread out over twenty thousand acres (about 8,100 hectares).

The Jicarilla have been endowed with beautiful land, and they are taking good care of it. They are more concerned with keeping healthy animal populations than are other agencies caring for wildlife. They are also sparing in how many hunters are allowed to harvest the herds. The bulk of harvest is hunting by tribal members. Jicarilla men, women, and children hunt in the fall, more for sustenance than for sport. A single elk can yield three hundred pounds (136 kilograms) of tasty meat, a real help in getting through the winter. The Jicarilla Fish and Game Department are modern conservation workers, and they are also upholding the values of Apaches through the generations in wisely caring for the health of Mother Earth.

Jicarilla and Mescalero Apache nations have both been able to generate healthy amounts of income from their resources. Not all Apache nations have been so fortunate. On several Apache reservations, unemployment is more than 50 percent. Many Apache people live below the *federal poverty level*. On the San Carlos Reservation, three out of every four members living on tribal lands are unemployed. Several Apache nations have land that is remote from cities and developers, making it difficult for them to move ahead financially.

A common problem among Apache tribes is the threat of lost languages. For years, federal Indian schools punished students for speaking their native language. Caucasian educators insisted that success in the modern world could only come if Indians lost their own language and culture. As a result of this attitude, younger generations were not taught their language.

Powwows are not an Apache tradition, but there are Apaches who participate in these inter-tribal events. They provide an opportunity to share cultures and make friends with Native people across North America.

Sociologists say that 50 percent of any culture is connected with its spoken language. If younger generations cannot speak the Ndee languages, they will not be able to carry on with the sacred traditions that have given strength to their tribes through the years.

At Mescalero, a recent survey found that two out of three tribal members could not speak the language. Jicarilla is similar. A survey of the White Mountain Apache found 95 percent of respondents forty years of age and over speak Apache, compared to only 41 percent of respondents age thirty-nine and under. On the San Carlos Apache Nation, 60 percent speak Apache, but one elder mourns that "the language is losing ground." The Lipan Apache who moved to Mexico and back were forced to keep their culture underground for many years. At present, Robert Soto and others are compiling a dictionary of Lipan words and researching ways to preserve their language.

Efforts are underway on all Apache nations to revitalize the native language. **Head Start** programs and reservation schools teach the languages.

In partnership with the University of New Mexico, the Jicarilla are developing a comprehensive dictionary. But it will take a dedicated effort by the young people for Apache nations to keep their ancestral dialects alive.

Indian nations are increasingly taking charge of their rights and resources to create a better future. At the same time, non-Indians need to abandon stereotyped thinking about their indigenous neighbors. The Apache have faced as much stereotyping as any group of people in North America. One way this persists is the use of the name "Apache" as school *mascots*.

The mascot issue is emotional. Students often feel attached to their school mascots. At the same time, there are compelling reasons to eliminate Indian mascots. Dr. Cornel Pewewardy, a Comanche-Kiowa professor of education, points out: "It should come as no surprise that non-Indian children programmed on these stereotypes at early ages grow into adults who may unwittingly or knowingly discriminate against Indians." Most Indian educational associations and tribal governments have stated their desire to eliminate Indian mascots and logos from school-related activities and events.

One school's use of "Apache" mascot became especially relevant to students at two schools—one in California and one on an Apache reservation. Arcadia High School in California received complaints about its mascot,

This mural in Dulce New Mexico reflects the forward-looking attitude of the Jicarilla Apache Nation.

Challenges for Today, Hopes for the Future 89

and the student council decided to communicate about the issue with the Alchesay High School on the White Mountain Apache Reservation in Arizona. The Arcadia principal traveled to Alchesay and heard students speak about the mascot issue. The *consensus* of Alchesay students was that Arcadia High School should not use the name "Apaches." One student told the Arcadia principal: "You've taken almost everything from us. In the very least, I ask that you leave us our name. Leave our heritage, our religion, our language, our ways, and our name alone."

Although Alchesay students were opposed to Arcadia's use of "Apache," the tribal council permitted the use of the name in a meeting with Arcadia's principal the next morning. So Arcadia retains the name. As a follow-up to their visit, a student group from Arcadia returned to White Mountain to deliver jackets and toys for children on the reservation. Students from Arcadia High met with Alchesay students, some in tears over the continuing use of "Apache" as the California school's mascot.

While the mascot issue is much talked about today, it is by no means new. Consider the following quotation:

> It seems that the world will never get rid of fakers . . . there have been, and are, a great many people using the Indians as their mascots. . . . Do they do any good? . . . They do more harm than good to the Indian people. . . . Anyone who poses as an Indian does not help the Indians.

These are the words of Carlos Montezuma, Yavapai Apache, and an influential Native American leader who graduated from the University of Illinois in 1884. He was a medical doctor who had a private practice and later taught medicine at a medical school.

The Apache-Ndee peoples continue to play an important role in North American life at the beginning of the twenty-first century. In politics, education, arts, and media, Apache people make significant contributions. On some reservations, Apache tribes are making notable economic gains. Yet other Apache nations struggle against poverty and the negative social problems that result. On some reservations, traditional languages and sacred customs struggle to continue.

On the San Carlos Reservation, Franklin Stanley Sr. affirms: "I speak, sing, and live my language." May many more Apache people be able to say the same, for many years to come. Grounded in their cultural identity, the Apache have much to offer us all.

Further Reading

Abdul-Jabbar, Kareem. *A Season on the Reservation: My Sojourn with the White Mountain Apache*. New York: William Morrow, 2000.

Barrett, S. M. (ed.). *Geronimo: His Own Story: The Autobiography of a Great Patriot Warrior*. New York: Meridian Books, 1996.

Roberts, David. *Once They Moved Like the Wind: Cochise, Geronimo, and the Apache Wars*. New York: Simon & Schuster, 1994.

Robinson, Sherry. *Apache Voices: Their Stories of Survival as Told to Eve Ball*. Albuquerque: University of New Mexico Press, 2000.

Tiller, Veronica E. Velarde. *The Jicarilla Apache Tribe: A History*. Albuquerque, N.M.: BowArrow Publishing, 2000.

Trimble, Stephen. *The People: Indians of the American Southwest*. Santa Fe, N.M.: SAR Press, 1993.

For More Information

Links to Apache Indians Sites by Phil Konstantin
members.tripod.com/~ PHILKON/links12apache.html

White Mountain Apache Tribe
www.wmat.nsn.us/

Home Site of the Jicarilla Apache Nation
www.jicarillaonline.com

San Carlos Apache Cultural Center
www.carizona.com/super/attractions/san_carlos.html

Welcome to the Yavapai-Apache Nation
www.yavapai-apache-nation.com

Lipan Apaches in Texas
www.texasindians.com/apach.htm

Publisher's Note:

The Web sites listed on this page were active at the time of publication. The publisher is not responsible for Web sites that have changed their address or discontinued operation since the date of publication. The publisher will review and update the Web sites upon each reprint.

Glossary

aboriginal: Relating to the first or earliest known of its kind in a region.

advocates: People who plead the cause of another.

apprenticeship: A period of service to someone skilled in a trade with the purpose of learning that trade or skill.

cabaret: A nightclub.

choreographer: The person who designs the movements of a dance.

Cochise: Chiricahua Apache Indian chief (1812?–1874).

conquistadors: Spanish conquerors.

consensus: A general agreement.

constitution: The laws, principles, and rules guiding a government or group.

diabetes: A disorder caused by an inadequate supply or utilization of insulin.

ecstatic: Feeling overwhelming delight.

epidemics: Diseases affecting a large number of people within a community.

evangelical: A Protestant religion with emphasis on the four Gospels and characterized by fundamentalism.

federal poverty level: The amount of personal or family income, established by the federal government, below which one is classified as poor.

genocide: The systematic destruction of a racial, political, or cultural group.

Head Start: A government preschool education program for children whose families meet financial guidelines.

HUD housing: A project of the federal government's Department of Housing and Urban Development to provide housing for people meeting certain guidelines.

icon: A pictorial representation of something.

indigenous: Naturally occurring in a particular area or environment.

jambalaya: Rice cooked with a variety of meats and seafood, and seasoned with herbs and spices.

mascots: People, animals, or objects adopted by a group to symbolize that group.

matriarchal: A society based on the mother as the head and ruler of the family and its descendents.

medicine man: Priestly healer.

mediums: Objects that can be used in the creation of artwork.

mesas: Isolated, relatively flat high land.

mescal: A small cactus.

nomadic: Having the characteristic of moving from place to place.

optimistic: Anticipate the best of a situation.

organic: Derived from living organisms.

poachers: People who trespass for the purpose of stealing something, usually game.

powwow: A Native American social gathering that highlights the culture and dance.

reggae: Popular music of Jamaican origin that combines native styles with elements of rock and roll and soul music.

reservation: A tract of land put aside for the use of Native Americans.

small pox: A contagious disease characterized by skin eruptions and scarring.

synthetic: Something produced artificially.

traditional: Having to do with a culture's inherited beliefs and customs.

tuberculosis: A contagious lung disease.

utilitarian: Something that can be used, is practical.

Vatican: The home of the Pope.

vigilante: Someone who takes the law into his own hands.

Westerners: People who advocate the adoption of western European ways.

Index

Abdul-Jabbar, Kareem 58–59
alcohol 36, 51, 59, 65
Aravaipa Apache 19, 30
Arizona 19, 30, 31, 45, 56, 59, 77

basket weaving 24, 72–74
buffalo 22, 24, 36, 64
burden baskets 72–73

Camp Grant massacre 19
Canada 20, 48
Caramillo, Lamavaya 38
Carson, Kit 22
casinos 22, 34, 36, 37
cattle 28, 30, 31, 55
Changing Woman, the 41, 42, 43, 44
Child of Water 13, 14–16, 17
Chino, Wendell 22, 32, 33–37, 78
Chiricahua Apache 12–13, 14, 21, 26–29, 30, 33, 39, 51, 62, 63, 75
Choctaw-Lipan Apache 23, 31
Cibecue Apache 29
clans 56, 57, 59
Cochise 27, 33, 39
Comanche 22, 24
constitution 28, 34, 37
Crown Dancers 40, 43
culture 31, 34, 59–60, 88
Curtis, Edward 17

diseases 22, 24, 25, 59, 65

education 37, 38, 86
Elote, Rowyn H. 67–68, 69

farming 24, 26, 30, 33, 64
Fort Sill 27, 28, 29, 33, 51, 63

Gaan 43, 44, 46, 49, 50
Geronimo 27, 28, 29, 33, 46, 51, 63
Go-Jii-Ya feast 60–61
Goyahkla 26–27, 28, 29

Haozous, Bob 65
horses 24, 55, 58, 64, 78
Houser, Allan 62, 63–65
HUD housing 59, 60

"Indian New Deal" 22
Indian relocation program 77, 78
Indian Reorganization Act of 1934 22, 25, 37
Institute of American Indian Arts 65, 66, 67

Jicarilla Apache 13, 16, 20, 22, 24–26, 27, 35, 36, 38, 39, 43, 55, 56, 60, 61, 67, 68, 70, 71, 74, 83, 84, 88, 89
Jicarilla Fish and Game Department 86–87

Kie, Laurence Jr. 38, 39
Kiowa Apache 20, 23–24, 48

language 12, 20, 29, 38, 59, 87–89, 90
Lipan Apache 13, 20, 22–23, 31, 48, 58, 88
Llanero band 20, 24, 35, 56, 60, 67

matriarchal clans 56, 57
Mazzio, Joann 33, 35
Medicine Lodge Treaty 24
medicine men and women 19, 43, 44, 45, 51
Mescalero Apache 20, 22, 23, 24, 28, 31, 33, 34, 35, 37, 46, 47, 56, 59, 64, 88
Mexico 22, 23, 28, 48, 58, 88
Misquez, Sara 37, 38
Montez, Amaurante 81
Montezuma, Carlos 90
Mount Graham 45–46

Native American Church 48
Navajo 21, 29, 37
New Mexico 16, 22, 24, 33, 35, 36, 39, 47, 56, 62, 64, 65, 67, 86
Nunez-Velarde, Shelden 68, 69–70, 71–72

oil 25, 35, 39, 84
Oklahoma 24, 27, 28, 29, 33, 48, 63, 64, 65
Ollero clan 24, 35, 56, 60, 67, 68, 69

Pentecostal churches 49, 51
powwows 76, 78, 88
Puberty Ceremony 41

reservation 22, 24, 28, 30, 31, 33, 36, 37, 45, 46, 47, 48–49, 51, 54, 58, 60, 61, 77, 86, 87, 90
rodeo performers 58, 67, 69

San Carlos Apache 29, 31, 39, 56, 75, 87, 88
San Carlos Apache Cultural Center 17, 18, 25, 73
Sanchez, Stacey 83–84
Sine, Duke Wasaaja 40, 42, 49, 50, 66, 82
Sisto, Earl 76, 77–78, 81
Soto, Robert 48, 88
sovereignty 34
Stanley, Franklin Sr. 75
stereotypes 11, 19, 20, 54, 89
Stevens, Herbert 12
Sunrise Dance 41–44, 59

tepees 20, 24, 61, 67
Tiller, Veronica 24
Titla, Mary Kim 78, 79, 81
Tonto Apaches 29, 30, 31
Trujillo, Raoul 79, 80, 81

unemployment 51, 86, 87
U.S. government 22, 24, 28, 29, 30, 31, 37, 77, 84

Velarde, Ollin 67, 68
Verde Valley Apache 29, 31
Vicenté, Eudané 87
Vigil, Augustin 38
Vigil, Nossman 38
Vigil-Muniz, Claudia 38–39

Western Apache 21, 29, 30, 31, 56
White Mountain Apache 29, 30, 31, 42, 53, 54, 56, 58–59, 88, 90
White Painted Woman 13–14, 41–42, 43
women, and community 54–56, 57
women, in government 37, 38, 39

Yavapai Apache 15, 31, 77, 90

Biographies

Kenneth McIntosh is a pastor and his wife, Marsha, is a schoolteacher. They both took leave from their regular jobs to work on this series. Formerly, Kenneth worked as a junior high teacher in Los Angeles, California. He wrote *Clergy* for the Mason Crest series "Careers with Character." The McIntoshes live in upstate New York and have two children, Jonathan and Eirené. They are grateful for the opportunity this work has given them to travel and meet with many wonderful Native people.

Martha McCollough received her bachelor's and master's degrees in anthropology at the University of Alaska-Fairbanks, and she now teaches at the University of Nebraska. Her areas of study are contemporary Native American issues, ethnohistory, and the political and economic issues that surround encounters between North American Indians and Euroamericans.

Benjamin Stewart, a graduate of Alfred University, is a freelance photographer and graphic artist. He traveled across North America to take the photographs included in this series.